SIDE BY SIDE

English
Through
Guided Conversations
1A

Steven J. Molinsky

Bill Bliss

Illustrated by

Richard E. Hill

Prentice-Hall Inc., Englewood Cliffs, New Jersey 07632

Library of Congress Cataloging in Publication Data

MOLINSKY, STEVEN J.
    Side by Side

    Includes indexes.
        1. English language—Conversation and phrase books.
    2. English language—Text books for foreign speakers.
    I. Bliss, Bill. II. Title.
    PE1131.M58 1983   428.3′4   82-20425
    ISBN 0-13-809715-1 (Book 1A)

Printed in the United States of America

10   9   8

Editorial/production supervisor: Penelope Linskey
Art/camera copy supervisor: Diane Heckler-Koromhas
Cover design by Suzanne Behnke
Manufacturing buyer: Harry P. Baisley

0-13-809715-1

PRENTICE-HALL INTERNATIONAL, INC., *London*
PRENTICE-HALL OF AUSTRALIA PTY. LIMITED, *Sydney*
EDITORA PRENTICE-HALL DO BRASIL, LTDA., *Rio de Janeiro*
PRENTICE-HALL OF CANADA, LTD., *Toronto*
PRENTICE-HALL OF INDIA PRIVATE LIMITED, *New Delhi*
PRENTICE-HALL OF JAPAN, INC., *Tokyo*
PRENTICE-HALL OF SOUTHEAST ASIA PTE. LTD., *Singapore*
WHITEHALL BOOKS LIMITED, WELLINGTON, *New Zealand*

Contents

BOOK 1A

To the Teacher

Side by Side is a conversational grammar book.

We do not seek to describe the language, or prescribe its rules. Rather, we aim to help students learn to *use* the language grammatically, through practice with meaningful conversational exchanges.

This book is intended for adult and young-adult learners of English. It is designed to provide the beginning student with the basic foundation of English grammar, through a carefully sequenced progression of conversational exercises and activities. Teachers of nonbeginning students will also find these materials to be effective as a rapid, concise review of basic structures of the language.

WHY A CONVERSATIONAL GRAMMAR BOOK?

Grammar is usually isolated and drilled through a variety of traditional structural exercises such as repetition, substitution, and transformation drills. These exercises effectively highlight particular grammatical structures . . . but they are usually presented as a string of single sentences, not related to each other in any unifying, relevant context.

Traditional dialogues, on the other hand, may do a fine job of providing examples of real speech, but they don't usually offer sufficient practice with the structures being taught. Teachers and students are often frustrated by the lack of a clear grammatical focus in these meaningful contexts. And besides that, it's hard to figure out what to *do* with a dialogue after you've read it, memorized it, or talked about it.

In this book we have attempted to combine the best features of traditional grammatical drills and contextually rich dialogues. We aim to actively engage our students in meaningful conversational exchanges within carefully structured grammatical frameworks. And we encourage our students to then break away from the textbook and *use* these frameworks to create conversations *on their own*.

While we have designed this text for the beginning student, we are also concerned about the nonbeginner. Although this student has made progress in understanding and using the language, he or she often needs more practice with the basics, the "nuts and bolts" of elementary English grammar.

(Intermediate-level teachers often tell us that even though their students are doing beautifully with the present perfect tense, they still have trouble with such "early" structures as the third-person singular -s or the difference between the simple present and present continuous tenses.)

This book offers nonbeginners the opportunity to use their richer vocabularies in open-ended conversational exercises which focus on the basic grammatical structures of the language.

AN OVERVIEW

GRAMMATICAL PARADIGMS

Each lesson in the book covers one or more specific grammatical structures. A new structure appears first in the form of a grammatical paradigm, a simple schema of the structure.

These paradigms are meant to be a reference point for students as they proceed through the lesson's conversational activities. While these paradigms highlight the structures being taught, we don't intend them to be goals in themselves.

We don't want our students simply to parrot back these rules: we want them to engage in conversations that show they can *use* them correctly.

GUIDED CONVERSATIONS

Guided conversations are the dialogues and the question and answer exchanges which are the primary learning devices in this book. Students are presented with a model conversation that highlights a specific aspect of the grammar. In the exercises that follow the model, students pair up and work "Side by Side," placing new content into the given conversational framework.

How to Introduce Guided Conversations

There are many alternative ways to introduce these conversations. We don't want to dictate any particular method. Rather, we encourage you to develop strategies that are compatible with your own teaching style, the specific needs of your students, and the particular grammar and content of the lesson at hand.

Some teachers will want books closed at this stage, so their students will have a chance to listen to the model before seeing it in print.

Other teachers will want students to have their books open for the model conversation or see it written on the blackboard. The teacher may read or act out the conversation while students follow along, or may read through the model with another student, or may have two students present the model to the class.

Whether books are open or closed, students should have ample opportunity to understand and practice the model before attempting the exercises that follow it.

How to Use Guided Conversations

In these conversational exercises, we are asking our students to place new content into the grammatical and contextual framework of the model. The numbered exercises provide the student with new information which is "plugged into" the framework of the model conversation. Sometimes this framework actually appears as a "skeletal dialogue" in the text. Other times the student simply inserts the new information into the model that has just been practiced. (Teachers who have written the model conversation on the blackboard can create the skeletal dialogue by erasing the words that are replaced in the exercises.)

The teacher's key function is to pair up students for "Side by Side" conversational practice, and then to serve as a resource to the class, for help with the structure, new vocabulary, and pronunciation.

"Side by Side" practice can take many forms. Most teachers prefer to call on two students at a time to present a conversation to the class. Other teachers have all their students pair up and practice the conversations with a partner. Or small groups of students might work together, pairing up within these groups and presenting the conversations to others in the group.

This paired practice helps teachers address the varying levels of ability of their students. Some teachers like to pair stronger students with weaker ones. The slower student clearly gains through this pairing, while the more advanced student also strengthens his or her abilities by lending assistance to the speaking partner.

Other teachers will want to pair up or group students of *similar* levels of ability. In this arrangement, the teacher can devote greater attention to students who need it, while giving more capable students the chance to learn from and assist each other.

While these exercises are intended for practice in conversation, teachers also find them useful as *writing* drills which reinforce oral practice and enable students to study more carefully the grammar highlighted in these conversations.

Once again, we encourage you to develop strategies that are most appropriate for your class.

The "Life Cycle" of a Guided Conversation

It might be helpful to define the different stages in the "life cycle" of a guided conversation.

1. *The Presentation Stage*
   The model conversation is introduced and practiced by the class.

2. *The Rehearsal Stage*
   Immediately after practicing the model, students do the conversational exercises that follow. For homework, they practice these conversations, and perhaps write out a few. Some lessons also ask students to create their own original conversations based on the model.

3. *The Performance Stage*
   The next day students do the conversational exercises in class, preferably with their textbooks and notebooks closed. Students shouldn't have to memorize these conversations. They will most likely remember them after sufficient practice in class and at home.

4. *The Incorporation Stage*
   The class reviews the conversation or pieces of the conversation in the days that follow. With repetition and time, the guided conversation "dissolves" and its components are incorporated into the student's active language.

ON YOUR OWN

An important component of each lesson is the "On Your Own" activity. These student-centered exercises reinforce the grammatical structures of the lesson while breaking away from the text and allowing students to contribute content of their own.

These activities take various forms: role-plays, interviews, extended guided conversations, and questions about the student's real world.

In these exercises, we ask students to bring to the classroom new content, based on their interests, their backgrounds, and the farthest reaches of their imaginations.

We recommend that the teacher read through these activities in class and assign them as homework for presentation the next day. In this way, students will automatically review the previous day's grammar while contributing new and inventive content of their own.

"On Your Own" activities are meant for simultaneous grammar reinforcement and vocabulary building. Beginning students will tend to recycle previous textbook vocabulary into these activities. While this repetition is clearly useful, beginners should also be encouraged to use other words which are familiar to them but are not in the text. *All* students should be encouraged to use a dictionary in completing the "On Your Own" activities. In this way, they will not only use the words they know, but the words they would *like* to know in order to really bring their interests, backgrounds, and imaginations into the classroom.

As a result, students will be teaching each other new vocabulary and also sharing a bit of their lives with others in the class.

CLASSROOM DRAMAS

"Classroom Dramas" are the full-page comic strip dialogues that appear every once in a while throughout the text. The goal of these dialogues is to tackle a specific grammatical structure and give students the opportunity to rehearse this structure in a short, playful classroom conversation.

Some teachers will simply want to read through these dramas with their students. Others might want to act them out, using students in the class as the characters.

Students enjoy memorizing these dramas and using them frequently throughout the course. In fact, they often break into these conversations spontaneously, without any prompting from the teacher. (Our students, for example, like to impress visitors to the class by confidently performing these dramas as though they were really happening for the first time.)

In conclusion, we have attempted to make the study of English grammar a lively and relevant experience for our students. While we hope that we have conveyed to you the substance of our textbook, we also hope that we have conveyed the spirit: that learning the grammar can be conversational . . . student-centered . . . and fun.

Steven J. Molinsky
Bill Bliss

To Be: Introduction

Read and practice.

Answer these questions.

1. What is your name?
   _____

2. What is your address?
   _____

3. What is your phone number?
   _____

4. Where are you from?
   _____

Now ask the other students in your class.

*Pronounce: two thirty-five.
†Pronounce: seven four one, eight nine "oh" six. (For
the complete list of numbers, see page xii.)

Interview a famous person. Make up addresses, phone numbers, and cities. Use your imagination. Role-play these interviews in class.

A. What is your name?

B. My name is _____ .

A. _____ address?

B. _____ .

A. _____ phone number?

B. _____ .

A. Where are you from?

B. _____ .

A. Thank you very much.

B. You're welcome.

a famous actor

a famous actress

a famous athlete

the president/prime minister of your country

To Be + Location
Subject Pronouns

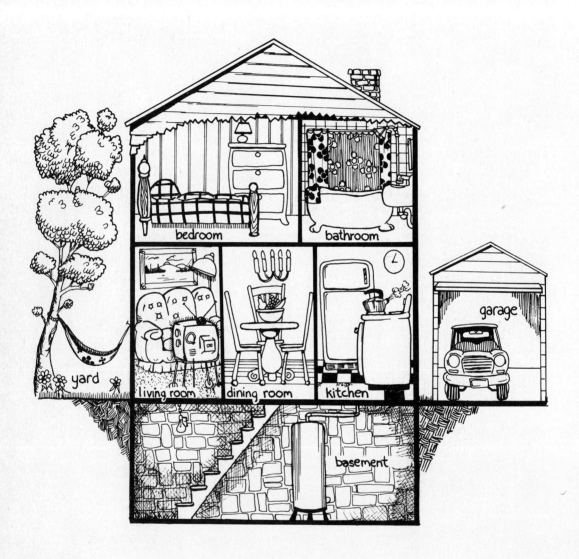

bedroom

bathroom

garage

living room

dining room

kitchen

yard

basement

I	am	I'm	
He		He's	
She } is		She's }	
It →		It's	in the kitchen.
We		We're	
You } are		You're }	
They		They're'	

	am	I	
		he	
	is	she	
		it	
Where			?
	are	we	
		you	
		they	

Read and practice.

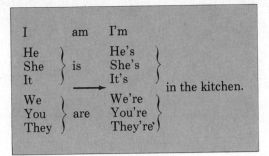

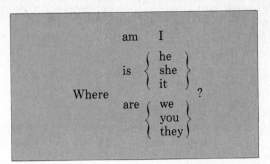

Answer these questions.

1. Where are you?

2. Where are you?

3. Where are you?

4. Where are you?

5. Where are Bill and Mary?

6. Where are Mr. and Mrs. Wilson?

7. Where are you?

8. Where are you and Tom?

9. Where are Mr. and Mrs. Johnson?

Read and practice.

*Where is → Where's

Answer these questions.

1. Where's Tom?

2. Where's Fred?

3. Where's Helen?

4. Where's Betty?

5. Where's the newspaper?

6. Where's the cat?

7. Where's Jane?

8. Where's John?

9. Where's the dog?

WHERE ARE THEY?

Ask and answer questions based on these pictures.

1. _____ Albert?
_____.

2. _____ Carmen?
_____.

3. _____ Walter and Mary?
_____.

4. _____ you?
_____.

5. _____ you?
_____.

6. _____ Rita?
_____.

7. _____ Mr. and Mrs. Jones?
_____.

8. _____ the monkey?
_____.

9. _____ I?
_____.

ON YOUR OWN

Add people and places of your own.

10. _____ ?
_____.

11. _____ ?
_____.

12. _____ ?
_____.

Present Continuous Tense

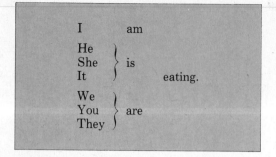

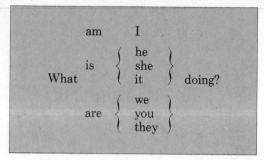

Read and practice.

*What is→what's.

Complete these conversations.

1. What are you doing?
   _____ reading the newspaper.

2. _____ Mr. and Mrs. Jones doing?
   _____ eating dinner.

3. _____ Henry doing?
   _____ cooking dinner.

4. _____ Maria doing?
   _____ studying English.

5. _____ Frank doing?
   _____ sleeping.

6. _____ Sam and Betty doing?
   _____ watching TV.

7. _____ Judy doing?
   _____ playing the piano.

8. What are YOU doing?
   I'm _____.

WHERE ARE THEY
AND WHAT ARE THEY DOING?

Ask and answer these questions.

1. Where's Walter?
   He's in the kitchen.
   What's he doing?
   He's eating breakfast.

2. _____ Betty?
   _____ park.
   _____ doing?
   _____ eating lunch.

3. _____ Mr. and Mrs. Smith?
   _____ dining room.
   _____ doing?
   _____ eating dinner.

4. _____ you?
   _____ bedroom.
   _____ doing?
   _____ playing the guitar.

5. _____ you?
   _____ living room.
   _____ doing?
   _____ playing cards.

6. _____ Tom and Mary?
   _____ yard.
   _____ doing?
   _____ playing baseball.

7. _____ Miss Jackson?
   _____ restaurant.
   _____ doing?
   _____ drinking coffee.

8. _____ Mr. Larson?
   _____ cafeteria.
   _____ doing?
   _____ drinking lemonade.

9. _____ you?
_____ library.
_____ doing?
_____ studying English.

10. _____ Tommy?
_____ classroom.
_____ doing?
_____ studying mathematics.

11. _____ Gloria?
_____ discotheque.
_____ doing?
_____ dancing.

12. _____ Harry?
_____ bathroom.
_____ doing?
_____ singing.

13. _____ Barbara?
_____ hospital.
_____ doing?
_____ watching TV.

14. _____ you?
_____ park.
_____ doing?
_____ listening to the radio.

ON YOUR OWN

Add people, places, and actions of your own.

15. _____ ?
_____ .
_____ ?
_____ .

16. _____ ?
_____ .
_____ ?
_____ .

To Be: Short Answers
Possessive Adjectives

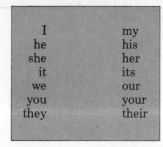

I	my
he	his
she	her
it	its
we	our
you	your
they	their

Read and practice.

	I	am.
Yes,	he she it	is.
	we you they	are.

Read and practice.

Are you busy?

Yes, I am.
I'm washing my hair.

Complete these conversations using the model above.

1. Is Nancy busy?
washing her car

3. Are you busy?
cleaning our yard

5. Are you busy?
doing my homework

2. Is Ted busy?
feeding his dog

4. Are Mr. and Mrs. Jones busy?
painting their kitchen

6. Is Peter busy?
doing his exercises

7. Is Linda busy?
fixing her bicycle

8. Are you busy?
cleaning our apartment

9. Are Bob and Judy busy?
washing their windows

10. Is Michael busy?
feeding his cat

11. Are you busy?
washing my clothes

12. Are you busy?
fixing our TV

13. Is Henry busy?
cleaning his garage

14. Are your children busy?
brushing their teeth

Use this model to talk about the picture above with other students in your class.

> **A.** Where's Miss Johnson?
>
> **B.** She's in the parking lot.
>
> **A.** What's she doing?
>
> **B.** She's washing her car.

To Be:
Yes/No Questions
Short Answers
Adjectives
Possessive Nouns

I	am	
He		
She	is	
It		tall.
We		
You	are	
They		

Read and practice.

Bob Bill

tall *short*

A. Is Bob tall or short?

B. He's tall.

A. Is Bill tall or short?

B. He's short.

Answer these questions.

Alice Margaret

young *old*

1. Is Alice young or old?

2. Is Margaret young or old?

Herman David

heavy
fat *thin*

3. Is Herman heavy or thin?

4. Is David fat or thin?

Herman's car David's car

new *old*

5. Is Herman's car new or old?

6. Is David's car new or old?

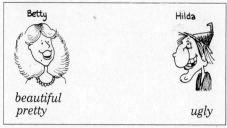

Betty Hilda

beautiful
pretty *ugly*

7. Is Betty beautiful or ugly?

8. Is Hilda pretty or ugly?

9. Is Edward handsome or ugly?

10. Is Captain Blood handsome or ugly?

11. Is Albert rich or poor?

12. Is John rich or poor?

13. Is Albert's house large or small?

14. Is John's apartment big or little?

15. Are Mary's neighbors noisy or quiet?

16. Are Jane's neighbors loud or quiet?

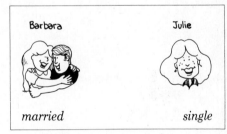

17. Is champagne expensive or cheap?

18. Is tea expensive or cheap?

19. Is Barbara married or single?

20. Is Julie married or single?

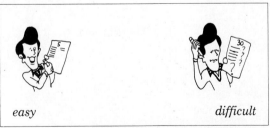

21. Are the questions in Chapter 5 easy or difficult?

22. Are the questions in Chapter 30 easy or difficult?

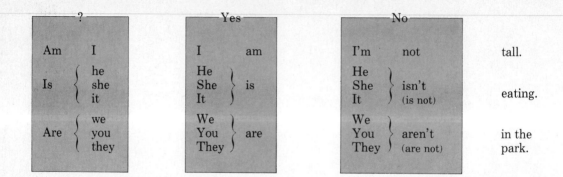

?			Yes			No		
Am	I		I	am		I'm	not	tall.
Is	he / she / it		He / She / It	is		He / She / It	isn't (is not)	eating.
Are	we / you / they		We / You / They	are		We / You / They	aren't (are not)	in the park.

Read and practice.

Answer these questions.

1. Tell me about your brother.

_____ _____ tall?

No, _____.

2. Tell me about your sister.

_____ _____ single?

No, _____.

3. Tell me about your apartment.

_____ _____ new?

No, _____.

4. Tell me about your new boss.

_____ _____ old?

No, _____.

5. Tell me about Stanley's Restaurant.

_____ _____ expensive?

No, _____.

6. Tell me about your neighbors.

_____ _____ noisy?

No, _____.

7. Tell me about Henry's cat.

_____ _____ pretty?

No, _____.

8. Tell me about Fred and Sally's dog.

_____ _____ little?

No, _____.

9. Tell me about the questions in your English book.

_____ _____ difficult?

No, _____.

10. Tell me about Santa Claus.

_____ _____ thin?

No, _____.

THE WEATHER

It's sunny.

It's cloudy.

It's raining.

It's snowing.

It's hot.

It's warm.

It's cool.

It's cold.

How's the weather today in YOUR city?

ON YOUR OWN

Read and practice.

A LONG-DISTANCE TELEPHONE CALL

A. Hi, Jack. This is Jim. I'm calling from Miami.

B. From Miami? What are you doing in Miami?

A. I'm on vacation.

B. How's the weather in Miami? Is it sunny?

A. No, it isn't. It's cloudy.

B. Is it hot?

A. No, it isn't. It's cold.

B. Are you having a good time?

A. No, I'm not. I'm having a TERRIBLE time. The weather is TERRIBLE here.

B. I'm sorry to hear that.

A. Hi, _____. This is _____. I'm calling from _____.

B. From _____? What are you doing in _____?

A. I'm on vacation.

B. How's the weather in _____? Is it _____?

A. No, it isn't. It's _____.

B. Is it _____?

A. No, it isn't. It's _____.

B. Are you having a good time?

A. No, I'm not. I'm having a TERRIBLE time. The weather is TERRIBLE here.

B. I'm sorry to hear that.

You're on vacation and the weather is terrible. Call a student in your class. Use the conversation above as a guide.

1. *Switzerland*
cool?
snowing?

2. *Honolulu*
hot?
sunny?

3. _____

Yes,	I	am.
	he / she / it	is.
	we / you / they	are.

No,	I'm not.	
	he / she / it	isn't.
	we / you / they	aren't.

Act this out in class.

YOU'RE A GENIUS!

To Be: Review

Read and practice.

MY FAVORITE PHOTOGRAPHS

A. Who is he?

B. He's my father.

A. What's his name?

B. His name is Paul.

A. Where is he (in this photograph)?

B. He's in Paris.

A. What's he doing?

B. He's standing in front of the Eiffel Tower.

Using these questions, talk about the photographs below.

Who is he/she? (Who are they?)
What _____ name (names)?
Where _____?
What _____ doing?

1. *my wife*
in New York
standing in front of the
Statue of Liberty

2. *my son*
in the park
playing soccer

3. *my daughter*
in her bedroom
sleeping

4. *my brother*
at the beach
swimming

5. *my sister and her husband*
at our house
standing in front of the fireplace

6. *my mother*
in our living room
sitting on the sofa and
watching TV

7. *my aunt and uncle*
in their dining room
having dinner

8. *my cousin*
in front of his house
washing his car

9. *my grandmother and grandfather*
at my wedding
crying

10. *my cousin*
in the park
sitting on a bench and
feeding the birds

11. *my friend*
sitting on his bed
playing the guitar

12. *my wife's brother**
in Washington
standing in front of the
Washington Monument

13. *my brother's wife†*
in their apartment
painting their living room

14. *my friends*
at my birthday party
singing and dancing

*Or: my brother-in-law.
†Or: my sister-in-law.

ON YOUR OWN

Bring in your favorite photographs.
Talk about them with other students
in your class. Ask the other students
about their favorite photographs.

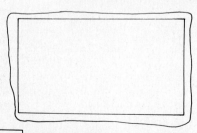

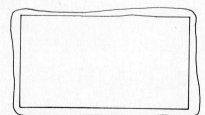

Prepositions
There Is/There Are
Singular/Plural:
Introduction

Read and practice.

Where's the restaurant?
It's **next to** the bank.

Where's the supermarket?
It's **across from** the movie theater.

Where's the school?
It's **between** the library and the park.

Where's the post office?
It's **around the corner from** the hospital.

1. Where's the park?

2. Where's the bank?

3. Where's the church?

4. Where's the movie theater?

5. Where's the restaurant?

6. Where's the police station?

7. Where's the fire station?

8. Where's the post office?

Read and practice.

A. Excuse me. Is there a laundromat in this neighborhood?*

B. Yes, there is. There's a laundromat on Main Street, next to the supermarket.

*You can say "in this neighborhood" or "nearby."

1. *post office?*

2. *bank?*

3. *movie theater?*

4. *gas station?*

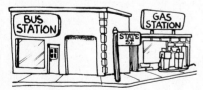

5. *bus station?*

6. *cafeteria?*

7. *drugstore?*

8. *library?*

| Is there . . . ? | Yes, there is. |
| | No, there isn't. |

Read and practice.

> Is there a restaurant in your neighborhood?

> No, there isn't.

> Is there a cafeteria in your neighborhood?

> Yes, there is.

> Where is it?

> It's on Central Avenue, across from the bank.

WHAT'S IN YOUR NEIGHBORHOOD?

Draw a simple map of your neighborhood. Pair off with another student in the class and ask each other about your neighborhoods. Here are some places you might want to include in your questions.

bakery	church	gas station	police station
bank	clinic	hospital	post office
barber shop	department store	laundromat	restaurant
beauty parlor	doctor's office	library	school
bus station	drugstore	movie theater	supermarket
cafeteria	fire station	park	train station

Singular		Plural	
a student a room an exercise	Yes, there is. No, there isn't.	students rooms exercises	Yes, there are. No, there aren't.

ON YOUR OWN

LOOKING FOR AN APARTMENT

You're looking for a new apartment. Another student in your class is the landlord. Ask the landlord about the apartment on page 39.

1. Is there a stove in the kitchen?
2. Is there a refrigerator in the kitchen?
3. Is there a superintendent in the building?
4. Is there an elevator in the building?
5. Is there a fire escape?
6. Is there a TV antenna on the roof?
7. Is there a radiator in every room?
8. Is there a mailbox near the building?
9. Is there a bus stop near the building?
10. Are there any pets in the building?
11. Are there any children in the building?
12. How many rooms are there in the apartment? (There are four rooms in the apartment.)
13. How many floors are there in the building?
14. How many closets are there in the bedroom?
15. How many windows are there in the living room?

Ask the landlord some other questions.

_____

_____

Are there any problems in the apartment on page 39? Don't ask the landlord! Another student in your class is a tenant in the building. Ask that student.

16. Are there any mice in the basement?
17. Are there any cockroaches in the apartment?
18. Are there any broken windows?
19. Are there any holes in the walls?

Ask the tenant some other questions.

_____

_____

_____

8

Singular/Plural
This/That/These/Those

Say these words after your teacher
and then place them in the chart
on the next page.

- hat
- glasses
- shirt
- tie
- jacket
- watch
- belt
- pants
- sock
- shoe

- earring
- necklace
- blouse
- bracelet
- skirt
- stocking

- coat
- glove
- pocketbook
- dress

- suit
- raincoat
- umbrella
- briefcase

- sweater
- mitten
- boot

Singular/Plural*

[s]	[z]	[iz]

[s]	[z]	[iz]
a book – books	a car – cars	a class – classes
a shop – shops	a school – schools	a church – churches
a student – students	a window – windows	a garage – garages
a bank – banks	a store – stores	an exercise – exercises
an airport – airports	an island – islands	an office – offices
a hat – hats		

*Some words have irregular plurals:

man – men
woman – women
child – children
person – people
tooth – teeth
mouse – mice

Colors

red	orange	yellow	green	blue	purple	black	brown
	pink	gray	white	gold	silver		

Read and practice.

IN THE DEPARTMENT STORE

A. May I help you?

B. Yes, please. I'm looking for a jacket.

A. Here's a nice jacket.

B. But this jacket is PURPLE!

A. That's O.K.* Purple jackets are very POPULAR this year.

*This is sometimes spelled: okay.

A. May I help you?

B. Yes, please. I'm looking for a _____.

A. Here's a nice _____.

B. But this _____ is _____!

A. That's O.K. _____ _____s are very POPULAR this year.

1. *green!*

2. *orange!*

3. *red!*

4. *yellow!*

5. *purple!*

6. *pink and green!*

7. *polka dot!*

8. *striped!*

Read and practice.

A. May I help you?

B. Yes, please. I'm looking for a pair of gloves.

A. Here's a nice pair of gloves.

B. But these gloves are GREEN!

A. That's O.K. Green gloves are very POPULAR this year.

A. May I help you?

B. Yes, please. I'm looking for a pair of _____.

A. Here's   nice pair of _____.

B. But these _____ are _____!

A. That's O.K. _____ _____s are very POPULAR this year.

---

1. *pink!*

2. *black!*

3. *red!*

4. *striped!*

5. *green and yellow!*

6. *purple and brown!*

7. *polka dot!*

8. *red, white, and blue!*

Talk about colors with the students in your class.

What are you wearing today?
What are the students in your class wearing today?
What's your favorite color?

Read and practice.

1. *pen*

2. *book*

3. *pencils*

4. *mittens*

5. *raincoat*

6. *earrings*

7. *sweater*

8. *boots*

Practice these conversations.

LOST AND FOUND

A. Is THIS your umbrella?

B. No, it isn't.

A. Are you sure?

B. Yes, I'm sure.
THAT umbrella is brown, and MY umbrella is black.

A. Are THESE your boots?

B. No, they aren't.

A. Are you sure?

B. Yes, I'm sure.
THOSE boots are dirty, and MY boots are clean.

Make up conversations, using colors and other adjectives you know.

1. *watch*

2. *glasses*

3. *pocketbook*

4. *gloves*

5. *little boy*

6. _____

Act this out, using names of students
in your class.

This/That

CLASSROOM DRAMA

Act this out, using names of students in your class.

These/Those

9

Simple Present Tense

I We You They } live.	Where do { I we you they } live?	What do { I we you they } do?

Read and practice.

Hello! My name is Antonio.
I live in Rome.
I speak Italian.

Every day

I eat Italian food,
I drink Italian wine,*
and I sing Italian songs.

I think Rome is a wonderful city.
I'm glad I live here.

*In practicing, you can say: coffee, tea, beer, etc.

INTERVIEWS AROUND THE WORLD

Interview these people, using the questions below.

What's your name?
Where do you live?
What language do you speak?
What do you do every day?

1. PARIS French Marie
2. MADRID Spanish Carlos
3. BERLIN German Frieda
4. TOKYO Japanese Toshi
5. LONDON English Sara and Mark
6. MOSCOW Russian Boris and Natasha

| He She It } lives. | Where does { he she it } live? | What does { he she it } do? |

Read and practice.

A. What's his name?

B. His name is Miguel.

A. Where does he live?

B. He lives in Mexico City.

A. What language does he speak?

B. He speaks Spanish.

A. What does he do every day?

B. He eats Mexican food,
he reads Mexican newspapers,
and he listens to Mexican music.

Ask and answer questions about these people.

What's his/her name?
Where does he/she live?
What language does he/she speak?
What does he/she do every day?

1.

2.

3.

4.

5.

6.

I We You They } live. He She } lives. It		Where	do { I we you they } does { he she it } live?	What	do { I we you they } does { he she it } do?

ON YOUR OWN

Interview a famous person.

A.   What's your name?

B.   _____ .

A.   _____ live?

B.   _____ .

A.   _____ speak?

B.   _____ .

A.   _____ every day?

B.   _____ .

Now tell the class about this person.

His/Her name is _____

_____

_____

_____

Simple Present Tense:
Yes/No Questions
Negatives
Short Answers

He cooks. He doesn't cook. (does not)	Does he cook? Yes, he does. No, he doesn't.	When What kind of food } does he cook?

STANLEY'S INTERNATIONAL RESTAURANT

Stanley's International Restaurant is a very special place.
Every day Stanley cooks a different kind of food.

Italian MONDAY	Greek TUESDAY	Chinese WEDNESDAY	Puerto Rican THURSDAY	Japanese FRIDAY	Mexican SATURDAY	American SUNDAY

What kind of food does Stanley cook on Monday?
     On Monday he cooks Italian food.

What kind of food does he cook on Tuesday? on Wednesday?
on Thursday? on Friday? on Saturday? on Sunday?

A. Does Stanley cook Greek food on Tuesday?

B. Yes, he does.

Ask five questions with "yes" answers.

A. Does Stanley cook Japanese food on Sunday?

B. No, he doesn't.

A. When does he cook Japanese food?

B. He cooks Japanese food on Friday.

Ask five questions with "no" answers.

You go. You don't go. (do not)	Do you go? Yes, I do. No, I don't.	When do you go?

A. Do you go to Stanley's International Restaurant on Wednesday?
B. Yes, I do.
A. Why?
B. Because I like Chinese food.

Ask these people.

1. *Friday*
  Japanese

2. *Saturday*
  Mexican

3. *Monday*
  Italian

4. *Thursday*
  Puerto Rican

A. Do you go to Stanley's International Restaurant on Sunday?
B. No, I don't.
A. Why not?
B. Because I don't like American food.

Ask these people.

5. *Monday*
  Italian

6. *Tuesday*
  Greek

7. *Wednesday*
  Chinese

8. *Saturday*
  Mexican

A. What kind of food do you like?
B. I like Russian food.
A. When do you go to Stanley's International Restaurant?
B. I don't go to Stanley's International Restaurant.
A. Why not?
B. Because Stanley doesn't cook Russian food.

Ask these people.

9. *French*   **10.** *German*   **11.** *Arabic*   **12.** *Hungarian*

What do people do at Stanley's International Restaurant?

On Monday they speak Italian, eat Italian food, drink Italian wine, smoke Italian cigarettes, and listen to Italian music.

1.

Henry likes Greek food.

> When does he go to Stanley's International Restaurant?
>
> What does he do there?

2.

Mr. and Mrs. Wilson go to Stanley's International Restaurant on Wednesday.

> What kind of food do they like?
>
> What do they do there?

Ask another student in your class.

When do you go to Stanley's International Restaurant?

Why?

What do you do there?

ON YOUR OWN

Answer these questions and then ask another student in your class.

1. **a.** What kind of movies do you like?
(Do you like comedies? dramas? westerns? war movies? science fiction? cartoons?)

   b. Who is your favorite movie actor? actress?

2. **a.** What kind of books do you like?
(Do you like novels? poetry? short stories?)

   b. Who is your favorite author?

3. What school subjects do you like?
(Do you like English? science? history? mathematics?)

4. **a.** What kind of TV programs do you like?
(Do you like comedies? dramas? westerns? cartoons?)

   b. Who is your favorite TV star?

5. What's your favorite food?

6. **a.** What kind of music do you like?
(Do you like classical music? popular music? jazz? rock and roll?)

   b. Who is your favorite singer?
(What kind of songs does he/she sing?)

7. **a.** Which sports do you like?
(Do you like football? baseball? soccer? golf? hockey? tennis?)

   b. Who is your favorite athlete?

CLASSROOM DRAMA

Yes, { I / we / you / they } do.	No, { I / we / you / they } don't.
{ he / she / it } does.	{ he / she / it } doesn't.

Act this out in class.

YOU SPEAK ENGLISH VERY WELL

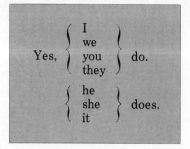
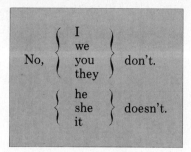

Object Pronouns
Simple Present Tense:
s vs. non-s endings
Adverbs of Frequency

I	me
he	him
she	her
it	it
we	us
you	you
they	them

Read and practice.

FRIENDS

Do you like me?

Of course I like you.
You're my friend.

1. Do you like John?
Of course I like him.
He's my friend.

2. Does John like you?
Of course he likes me.
I'm his friend.

3. Do you like Mary?
Of course I like her.
She's my friend.

4. Does Mary like you?
Of course she likes me.
I'm her friend.

5. Do you like Bob and Betty?
Of course I like them.
They're my friends.

6. Do Bob and Betty like you?
Of course they like me.
I'm their friend.

7. Do you like Bob and Betty?
Of course we like them.
They're our friends.

8. Do Bob and Betty like you?
Of course they like us.
We're their friends.

**Now try this using the names of
students in your class.**

[s]		[z]		[iz]			
sit	sits	read	reads	watch	watches	always	100%
help	helps	feed	feeds	dance	dances	usually	90%
look	looks	love	loves	wash	washes	sometimes	50%
think	thinks	go	goes	fix	fixes	rarely	10%
talk	talks					never	0%

Read and practice.

HARRY! I'M REALLY UPSET!

1. When we sit in the living room, you always watch TV and never look at me.
2. When we eat breakfast together, you always read the newspaper and never talk to me.
3. When we go to parties, you usually sit with your friends and rarely dance with me.
4. And you're lazy! You never help me.
5. When our windows are dirty, you never wash them.
6. When our car is broken, you never fix it.
7. And when our cats are hungry, you never feed them.
8. Sometimes I think you don't love me.

WHY IS SHE UPSET WITH HARRY?

1. When they sit in the living room he always _____.
2. _____.
3. _____.
4. _____.
5. _____.
6. _____.
7. _____.
8. _____.

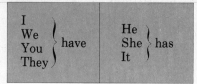

Read and practice.

DO YOU LOOK LIKE YOUR BROTHER?

My brother and I look very different.

I have brown eyes and he has blue eyes.
We both have brown hair, but I have short,
curly hair and he has long, straight hair.
I'm tall and thin. He's short and heavy.

No, I don't look like my brother. We look very different.

ON YOUR OWN

Answer these questions.

1. **Who Do You Look Like?**

   I look like _____.

   We're both _____.
   We both have _____.

2. **Who DON'T You Look Like?**

   I don't look like _____.

   _____.
   _____.
   _____.

Read and practice.

MY SISTER AND I ARE VERY DIFFERENT

My sister and I are very different.

I'm a teacher. She's a journalist.
I live in Chicago. She lives in Paris.
I have a small house in the suburbs. She has a large
apartment in the city.
I'm married. She's single.
I play golf. She plays tennis.
I play the piano. She doesn't play a musical instrument.
On the weekend I usually watch TV and rarely go out. She
never watches TV and always goes to parties.

We're very different. But we're sisters . . . and we're friends.

ON YOUR OWN

Compare yourself with a member of your family, another student in the class, or a famous person.

_____ and I Are Very Different

a.	(occupation?)	I _____	He/She _____
b.	(city?)	_____	_____
c.	(house? apartment?)	_____	_____
d.	(single? married? divorced?)	_____	_____
e.	(play a sport?)	_____	_____
f.	(play an instrument?)	_____	_____
g.	(on the weekend?)	_____	_____

Contrast:
Simple Present and
Present Continuous Tenses

Why Are You Crying?

I'm crying because I'm sad.
I ALWAYS cry when I'm sad.

1. Why are you smiling?

_____ happy.

I ALWAYS _____.

2. Why is he shouting?

_____ angry.

He ALWAYS _____.

3. Why is she smoking?

_____ nervous.

She ALWAYS _____.

4. Why is it drinking?

_____ thirsty.

It ALWAYS _____.

5. Why are they going to Stanley's Restaurant?

_____ hungry.

They ALWAYS _____.

6. Why is he going to the doctor?

_____ sick.

He ALWAYS _____.

7. Why are they shivering?

_____ cold.

They ALWAYS _____.

8. Why are you perspiring?

_____ hot.

I ALWAYS _____.

9. Why is she yawning?

_____ tired.

She ALWAYS _____.

10. Why is he blushing?

_____ embarrassed.

He ALWAYS _____.

What do you do when you're nervous?

Do you smoke?

Do you perspire?

Do you bite your nails?

Answer these questions and then ask another student in your class.

What do you do when you're . . .

1. nervous?   When I'm nervous I bite my nails.

2. sad?

3. happy?

4. tired?

5. sick?

6. cold?

7. hot?

8. hungry?

9. thirsty?

10. angry?

11. embarrassed?

Read and practice this conversation.

A. What are you doing?!

B. I'm washing the dishes in the bathtub.

A. That's strange! Do you USUALLY wash the dishes in the bathtub?

B. No. I NEVER wash the dishes in the bathtub, but I'm washing the dishes in the bathtub TODAY.

A. Why are you washing the dishes in the bathtub?

B. Because my SINK is broken.

A. I'm sorry to hear that.

A. What are you doing?!

B. I'm _____.

A. That's strange!   Do you USUALLY _____?

B. No, I NEVER _____, but I'm _____ TODAY.

A. Why are you _____?

B. Because my _____ is broken.

A. I'm sorry to hear that.

1. sleep
  sleeping } *on the floor*
  bed

2. cook
  cooking } *on the radiator*
  stove

3. study
  studying } *English by candlelight*
  lamp

4. shout
  shouting } *to my neighbor across
  the street*
  telephone

5. hitchhike
  hitchhiking } *to work*
  car

6.

13

Can
Have to

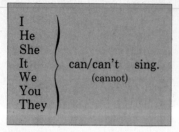

I	
He	
She	
It	can/can't sing.
We	(cannot)
You	
They	

Can you sing?
Yes, I can.
No, I can't.

Read and practice.

Can you speak Hungarian?

No, I can't. But I can speak English.

UNITED NATIONS

1. Can Mary ski? **2.** Can Sam cook Chinese food?

3. Can they play the violin? **4.** Can you sing?

CHESS CHECKERS

5. Can Jeff play chess? **6.** Can William play the piano?

7. Can Sally play football? **8.** Can they skate?

9. Ask another student in your class: Can you _____?

Read and practice.

A. Can Jack fix cars?

B. Of course he can.
He fixes cars every day. He's a mechanic.

1. Can Arthur play the violin?
violinist

2. Can Anita sing?
singer

3. Can Fred and Ginger dance?
dancer

4. Can Stanley cook?
chef

5. Can Lois bake apple pies?
baker

6. Can Richard act?
actor

7. Can Elizabeth and Katherine act?
actress

8. Can Eleanor teach?
teacher

9. Can Shirley drive a truck?
truck driver

10. Can Dan drive a bus?
bus driver

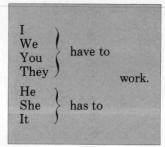

I	
We	have to
You	
They	work.
He	
She	has to
It	

Herbert is depressed. He's having a party today, but his friends can't go to his party. They're all busy.

A. Can Michael go to Herbert's party?

B. No, he can't. He has to go to the doctor.

1. *Peggy?*
fix her car

2. *George and Martha?*
go to the supermarket

3. *Nancy?*
go to the dentist

4. *Henry?*
clean his apartment

5. *Carl and Tim?*
do their homework

6. *Linda?*
wash her clothes

7. *Ted?*
go to the bank

8. Can YOU go to Herbert's party?

No, _____.

76

Read and practice.

Tom. Can you go to a movie with me on Friday?

I'm sorry. I can't. I have to do my laundry.

Sara. Can you go skating with me on Wednesday?

I'm sorry. I can't. I have to go to the dentist.

_____. Can you _____ with me on _____?

I'm sorry. I can't. I have to _____.

Make up conversations with other students in your class.

Include some of these words in your questions.

go to a movie
go to a baseball game
have lunch
have dinner
go swimming
go dancing
go skating
go skiing
go shopping
go bowling
go sailing
go jogging

Include some of these words and others in your answers.

go to the doctor
go to the bank
do my homework
visit a friend in the hospital
work
_____
_____
_____
_____
_____
_____
_____

Future: Going to
Time Expressions
Want to

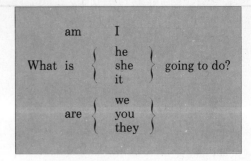

I	am	
He		
She	is	going to read.
It		
We		
You	are	
They		

What	is	he / she / it	going to do?
	am	I	
	are	we / you / they	

Read and practice.

A. What's Fred going to do today?*

B. He's going to fix his car.

A. What are Mr. and Mrs. Brown going to do tomorrow?†

B. They're going to go to the beach.

today includes:

this morning
this afternoon
this evening
tonight

† *tomorrow* includes:

tomorrow morning
tomorrow afternoon
tomorrow evening
tomorrow night

1. What's Mary going to do this morning?

2. What are Carol and Dan going to do tomorrow morning?

3. What are you going to do this afternoon?

4. What's Tom going to do tomorrow afternoon?

5. What are Mr. and Mrs. Smith going to do this evening?

6. What's Jane going to do tomorrow evening?

7. What are you going to do tonight?

8. What's Henry going to do tomorrow night?

9. Ask another student: What are you going to do _____?
(tomorrow, this evening…)

Read and practice.

*Other phrases you can use are:

this/next week, month, year

this/next Sunday, Monday, Tuesday, Wednesday, Thursday, Friday, Saturday

this/next January, February, March, April, May, June, July, August, September, October, November, December

this/next spring, summer, fall (autumn), winter

†"Right away," "immediately," and "at once" mean the same as "right now."

1. When are you going to wash your car?

2. When are you going to call your grandmother?

3. When are you going to visit us?

4. When are you going to cut your hair?

5. When are you going to plant flowers this year?

6. When are you going to fix your car?

7. When are you going to write to your Uncle John?

8. Mr. Smith! When are you going to iron those pants?

9. Ask another student: When are you going to _____?

I			
We	want to		
You			
They			study.
He			
She	wants to		
It			

Read and practice.

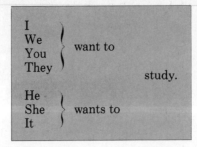

A. What are you going to do tomorrow?

B. I don't know.
I want to **go swimming,** but I think the weather is going to be bad.

A. Really? What's the forecast?

B. The radio says it's going to **rain.**

A. That's strange! According to the newspaper, it's going to **be sunny.**

B. I hope you're right.
I REALLY want to **go swimming.**

1. *have a picnic*
   rain
   be nice

2. *go skiing*
   be warm
   snow

3. *go to the beach*
   be cloudy
   be sunny

4. *plant flowers in my garden*
   be very hot
   be cool

5. *go sailing*
   be foggy
   be clear

6. *go to the zoo with my children*
   be cold
   be warm

Discuss in class.

What's the weather today?
What's the weather forecast for tomorrow?

WHAT TIME IS IT?

It's 11:00.   It's eleven o'clock.

It's 11:15.   It's eleven fifteen.*

It's 11:30.   It's eleven thirty.*

It's 11:45.   It's eleven forty-five.*

It's 12:00.   It's twelve o'clock.

 noon   midnight

ON YOUR OWN

Read and practice this conversation.

A. What time does the concert begin?

B. It begins at 8:00.

A. Oh no! I think we're going to be late!

B. Why? What time is it?

A. It's 7:30. And we have to leave RIGHT NOW!

B. I can't leave now. I'm SHAVING!

A. Please try to hurry! I don't want to be late for the concert.

*You can also say:

11:15 — a quarter after eleven
11:30 — half past eleven
11:45 — a quarter to twelve

A. What time does _____?

B. It _____ at _____.

A. Oh no! I think we're going to be late!

B. Why? What time is it?

A. It's _____. And we have to leave RIGHT NOW!

B. I can't leave now. I'm _____!

A. Please try to hurry! I don't want to be late for the _____.

1. What time does the football game begin?
2:00/1:30
taking a bath

2. What time does the plane leave?
4:15/3:45
putting on my clothes

3. What time does the English class begin?
9:00/8:45
getting up

4. What time does the bus leave?
7:00/6:30
packing my suitcase

5. What time does the train leave?
5:15/4:30
taking a shower

6. What time does the play begin?
8:30/8:00
looking for my pants

7. _____

Past Tense:
Regular Verbs
Introduction to
Irregular Verbs

HOW DO YOU FEEL TODAY?

I feel great!

I'm glad to hear that.

I feel fine.

I feel O.K.

So-so.

I'm sorry to hear that.

Not so good.

I feel terrible.

What's the matter with him?
He has a headache.

Ask and answer these questions.

 stomachache

toothache

backache

1. _____?
She _____.

2. _____?
He _____.

3. _____?
I _____.

earache

 sore throat

cold

4. _____?
He _____.

5. _____?
I _____.

6. _____?
She _____.

Ask another student in your class.

A. How do you feel today?
B. _____.
A. I'm glad to hear that.

A. How do you feel today?
B. _____.
A. What's the matter with you?
B. I have _____.
A. I'm sorry to hear that.

Yesterday I worked.	I work every day.
Yesterday I played the piano.	I play the piano every day.
Yesterday I rested.	I rest every day.

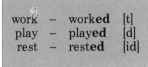

work	–	work**ed**	[t]
play	–	play**ed**	[d]
rest	–	rest**ed**	[id]

WHAT DID YOU DO YESTERDAY?

[t]

1. *I worked* 2. *cook* 3. *talk on the telephone* 4. *fix*

5. *brush* 6. *dance* 7. *smoke* 8. *watch*

[d]

9. *play* 10. *study* 11. *shave* 12. *smile*

13. *clean* 14. *cry* 15. *listen to* 16. *yawn*

[id]

17. *shout* 18. *paint* 19. *wait for* 20. *plant*

Every Day	Yesterday

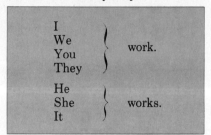
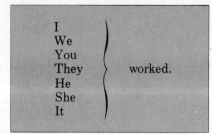

I We You They	work.	I We You They He She It	worked.
He She It	works.		

Read and practice.

A. How does John feel?
B. Not so good.
A. What's the matter with him?
B. He has a **sore throat**.
A. Why?
B. Because he **smoked** all day.*

*Or: all morning, all afternoon, all evening, all night.

1. *Mary*

2. *George*

3. *you*

4. *Fred*

5. *Mrs. Smith*

6. *you*

7. *David*

8. *you*

9. *Barbara*

Irregular Verbs

eat – ate	sing – sang	drink – drank	sit – sat

10. *Sally*

11. *Mario*

12. *you*

13. *Helen*

14. *you*

15. *Walter*

ON YOUR OWN

You don't feel very well today. Call
your doctor and make an appointment.

A. Hello, Doctor _____. This is _____.

B. Hello, _____. How are you?

A. I don't feel very well today.

B. I'm sorry to hear that. What seems to be the problem?

A. I have a TERRIBLE _____.

A. Well, Doctor . . . I probably have a terrible _____ because I _____ all _____ yesterday.

B. Do you USUALLY _____ all _____?

A. No, I don't. But I _____ all _____ YESTERDAY!

B. Do you want to make an appointment?

A. Yes, I do. When can you see me?

B. How about tomorrow at _____ o'clock?

A. That's fine. Thank you very much.

B. See you tomorrow.

A. Good-bye.

Past Tense:
Yes/No Questions
WH Questions
More Irregular Verbs

| I worked.
I didn't work.
(did not) | Did you work?
Yes, I did.
No, I didn't. |

Read and practice.

Did you brush your hair this morning*?

No, I didn't. I brushed my teeth.

*Today includes: Yesterday includes:

this morning   yesterday morning
this afternoon   yesterday afternoon
this evening   yesterday evening
tonight   last night

1. Did he study English last night?

2. Did she wash her windows this morning?

3. Did you play the piano yesterday afternoon?

4. Did they call the doctor this afternoon?

5. Did she listen to records yesterday morning?

6. Did he clean his bedroom today?

Read and practice.

1. Did you go skating yesterday?

go — went

2. Did you take the subway this morning?

take — took

3. Did Steven get up at 10:00 this morning?

get — got

4. Did he have a stomachache last night?

have — had

5. Did Mrs. Smith buy bananas yesterday?

buy — bought

6. Did Tommy write to his grandmother this week?

write — wrote

7. Did you read a book this afternoon?

read — read

8. Did they do their homework last night?

do — did

Read and practice.

1. Mary went to a party last night.

2. She got up late today.

3. She missed the bus.

4. She had to walk to the office.

5. She arrived late for work.

6. Her boss shouted at her.

7. She had a terrible headache all afternoon.

Complete this conversation, using the information above.

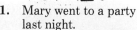

A. Hi, Mary! Did you have a good day today?

B. No, I didn't. I had a TERRIBLE day.

A. What happened?

B. I had a terrible headache all afternoon.

A. Why did you have a terrible headache all afternoon?

B. Because my boss shouted at me.

A. Why did your boss shout at you?

B. Because I arrived late for work.

A. Why _____ late for work?

B. Because _____.

A. Why _____?

B. Because _____.

A. Why _____?

B. Because _____.

A. Why _____?

B. Because I went to a party last night.

Ask another student in your class.

1. Did you go to a party last night?
2. What did you do last night?
3. Did you get up late today?
4. What time did you get up?
5. How did you get to class today?
6. Did you arrive on time?

**More
Irregular Verbs**

forget	–	forgot
meet	–	met
steal	–	stole

"EXCUSES! EXCUSES!"

Are you sometimes late for class?
What do you usually tell your teacher?
Here are some excuses you can use next time you're late.

I got up late.

I missed the _____. (bus, train, subway)

I had a _____ this morning. (stomachache, headache . . .)

I had to go to the _____ before class. (post office, bank, doctor, dentist . . .)

I forgot my _____ and had to go back home and get it. (English book, pencil . . .)

I met _____ on the way to class. (an old friend, my cousin . . .)

A thief stole my _____. (car, bicycle . . .)

Add some of your own excuses.

_____

_____

_____

Read and practice.

A. Why are you late for class?
Did you get up late?

B. No, I didn't get up late.

A. Did you have a headache this morning?

B. No, I didn't have a headache this morning.

A. Did you miss the bus?

B. No, I didn't miss the bus.

A. Well, why are you late for class?

B. A thief stole my bicycle.

A. Excuses! Excuses!

Now try this conversation with students in your class, using your own excuses.

A. Why are you late for class?
Did _____?

B. No, _____.

A. Did _____?

B. No, _____.

A. Did _____?

B. No, _____.

A. Well, why are you late for class?

B. _____.

A. Excuses! Excuses!

To Be: Past Tense

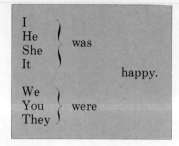

I
He
She } was
It
             happy.
We
You } were
They

Read and practice this commercial for WHAMMO Vitamins.

Before our family bought WHAMMO Vitamins, we were always tired.

I was tired.
My wife was tired.
My children were tired, too.

Now we're energetic, because WE bought WHAMMO Vitamins. How about you?

WHAMMO Commercial

Before our family bought _____,

we were always _____.

I was _____.

My wife/husband was _____.

My children were _____, too.

Now we're _____ because WE bought _____.

How about you?

Using the above script, prepare commercials for these other fine WHAMMO products.

1. *sad*   *happy*   2. *hungry*   *full*   3. *dirty*   *clean*

4. *sick*   *healthy*   5. *heavy*   *thin*   6. _____   _____

Before I bought WHAMMO Shampoo, my hair **was** always dirty. Now **it's** clean.

1. Before we bought WHAMMO Toothpaste, our teeth _____ yellow. Now _____ white.

2. Before we bought WHAMMO Paint, our house _____ ugly. Now _____ beautiful.

3. Before I bought WHAMMO Furniture, I _____ uncomfortable. Now _____ very comfortable.

4. Before we bought WHAMMO Dog Food, our dog _____ tiny. Now _____ enormous.

5. Before William bought WHAMMO Window Cleaner, his windows _____ dirty. Now _____ clean.

6. Before Mr. and Mrs. Brown bought WHAMMO Floor Wax, their kitchen floor _____ dull. Now _____ shiny.

7. Before I bought _____,

_____.

Now _____.

| I He She It | } | wasn't (was not) |
| We You They | } | weren't (were not) |

Read and practice.

A. Were you at the ballgame last night?

B. No, I wasn't. I was at the movies.

1. Was it hot yesterday?

2. Were they at home this morning?

3. Was Betty sad yesterday?

4. Was your grandfather a dentist?

5. Were you at home last weekend?

6. Was I a quiet baby?

7. Was Richard on time for his plane?

8. Was Nancy late for the bus?

I He She It We You They } did/didn't	I He She It } was/wasn't We You They } were/weren't

Read and practice.

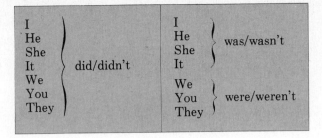

A. Did Tom have a big breakfast today?
B. Yes, he did. He was hungry.

A. Did Jane have a big breakfast today?
B. No, she didn't. She wasn't hungry.

1. Did you sleep well last night?

Yes, _____ tired.

2. Did Roger sleep well last night?

No, _____ tired.

3. Did Mrs. Brown go to the doctor yesterday?

Yes, _____ sick.

4. Did Mr. Brown go to the doctor yesterday?

No, _____ sick.

5. Did Timothy finish his milk?

Yes, _____ thirsty.

6. Did Jennifer finish her milk?

No, _____ thirsty.

7. Did Susan miss the train?

Yes, _____ late.

8. Did Sally miss the train?

No, _____ late.

Yes,	$\begin{Bmatrix} I \\ he \\ she \\ it \end{Bmatrix}$ was $\begin{Bmatrix} we \\ you \\ they \end{Bmatrix}$ were	No,	$\begin{Bmatrix} I \\ he \\ she \\ it \end{Bmatrix}$ wasn't $\begin{Bmatrix} we \\ you \\ they \end{Bmatrix}$ weren't

Yes,	$\begin{Bmatrix} I \\ he \\ she \\ it \\ we \\ you \\ they \end{Bmatrix}$ did	No,	$\begin{Bmatrix} I \\ he \\ she \\ it \\ we \\ you \\ they \end{Bmatrix}$ didn't

ON YOUR OWN

Answer these questions and then
ask other students in your class.

DO YOU REMEMBER YOUR CHILDHOOD?

1. What did you look like?
   Were you tall? thin? pretty? handsome? cute?
   Did you have curly hair? straight hair? long hair?
   Did you have dimples? freckles?

2. Did you have many friends?
   What did you do with your friends?
   What games did you play?

3. Did you like school?
   Who was your favorite teacher? Why?
   What was your favorite subject? Why?

4. What did you do in your spare time?
   Did you have a hobby?
   Did you play sports?

5. Who was your favorite hero?

6. How old were you when you began to talk?
   I was _____ years old when I began to talk.
   What were your first words?
   My first words were _____.

7. How old were you when you began to walk?

8. How old were you when you started school?

9. How old were you when you went on your first date?

Add three questions of your own and
ask other students in your class.

10. _____?
11. _____?
12. _____?

APPENDIX

Cardinal Numbers
Ordinal Numbers
Irregular Verbs:
Past Tense

Cardinal Numbers

1	one	13	thirteen	20	twenty
2	two	14	fourteen	21	twenty-one
3	three	15	fifteen	22	twenty-two
4	four	16	sixteen	.	.
5	five	17	seventeen	.	.
6	six	18	eighteen	29	twenty-nine
7	seven	19	nineteen	30	thirty
8	eight			40	forty
9	nine			50	fifty
10	ten			60	sixty
11	eleven			70	seventy
12	twelve			80	eighty
				90	ninety

100	one hundred	1,000	one thousand
200	two hundred	2,000	two thousand
300	three hundred	3,000	three thousand
.	.	.	.
.	.	.	.
		10,000	ten thousand
.	.	100,000	one hundred thousand
900	nine hundred	1,000,000	one million

Ordinal Numbers

1st	first	13th	thirteenth	20th	twentieth
2nd	second	14th	fourteenth	21st	twenty-first
3rd	third	15th	fifteenth	22nd	twenty-second
4th	fourth	16th	sixteenth	.	.
5th	fifth	17th	seventeenth	.	.
6th	sixth	18th	eighteenth	29th	twenty-ninth
7th	seventh	19th	nineteenth	30th	thirtieth
8th	eighth			40th	fortieth
9th	ninth			50th	fiftieth
10th	tenth			60th	sixtieth
11th	eleventh			70th	seventieth
12th	twelfth			80th	eightieth
				90th	ninetieth

one hundredth

one thousandth

one millionth

How to read a date:

June 9, 1941 = "June ninth, nineteen forty-one"

Irregular Verbs: Past Tense

be	was		light	lit
begin	began		lose	lost
bite	bit		make	made
break	broke		meet	met
bring	brought		put	put
buy	bought		read	read
catch	caught		ride	rode
come	came		run	ran
cut	cut		say	said
do	did		see	saw
drink	drank		sell	sold
drive	drove		send	sent
eat	ate		shake	shook
fall	fell		sing	sang
feed	fed		sit	sat
feel	felt		sleep	slept
fight	fought		speak	spoke
find	found		stand	stood
fly	flew		steal	stole
forget	forgot		sweep	swept
get	got		swim	swam
give	gave		take	took
go	went		teach	taught
grow	grew		tell	told
have	had		think	thought
hear	heard		throw	threw
hurt	hurt		understand	understood
know	knew		wear	wore
lead	led		write	wrote
leave	left			

Index

Word List

The number after each word indicates the page where the word first appears.

(adj) = adjective,   (n) = noun,   (pro) = pronoun,   (v) = verb